Sexual Lust, Demons, And Impurity

Johannes Tefo

Published by Johannes Tefo, 2024.

Also by Johannes Tefo

Family spiritual Warfare Books
Generational Curses And Spiritual Warfare: Spiritual Strategies & Principles Of Victory Against Evil Strongholds
Youth's Guide To Spiritual Warfare
A Women's Guide To Spiritual Warfare

Standalone
Deliver Your Soul From Evil
Overcoming Spirit Of Stagnation
The 24: Prophetic Word For This Season 2024 And Beyond
Michael For Warfare
Territorial Spirits: Overcome Evil Strongholds in Your Life And Take Over Your Community With Strategic Warfare And Winning Prayers
Prayers Against Suicide Spirit
Spiritual Warfare When Enough is Enough
Identity In Christ
Prayers Against Satanic Networks
The Workplace You Need: Spiritual Warfare Prayers That Silence Evil Powers At Your Workplace.
Deliverance From Mind Control: Be Free And Delivered From Every Marine Demons Of Mind Control
Times Getting Hard: Scriptures Of Comfort For Hard Days

Battle In The Sea: How To Tackle Spiritual Warfare And Win The Battle
Freedom: Deliverance Of Souls From Captivity
A Dedicated Prayer Lifestyle: Simple Tips To Effective Prayer Lifestyle
Deliverance From Sexual Dreams
Sexual Lust, Demons, And Impurity
Redefined By Fire: Unleashing The Power Of The Holy Spirit Within.

Table of Contents

Introduction.

S ince the time of Adam and Eve, men and women have struggled with sexual sin. The Canaanites were not immune to this. God drove them out because of the works of flesh such as homosexuality, bestiality, sexual immorality, and strange flesh, meaning, going after all sorts of animals to mate with them.

I don't know any other sin that has rampaged the world more than sexual immorality. A man and a woman of dignity and integrity can be seen in how he or she carries herself—fleeing from sexual immorality. I don't matter if you are the greatest leader or a prestigious being, if you are ever caught in immoral behavior sexually, people automatically lose respect for you.

Many men and women of God, the world has written off, while God cannot write you off, it is still difficult to earn the people you lead trust again. Spiritual people know that one thing that can demise your power, your authority in spirit, and your spiritual gifts, is when you are a loose man or woman sexually.

A man is a spirit, soul, and body. The works of the flesh come from the lust of the eye, the lust of the flesh, and the pride of life. We all know that Lucifer was demoted because of pride. Pride does not come from God.

Many times we fail because we approach issues from the surface, not from the roots. As a man is called a spirit before soul, and soul before body, then it means we ought to approach life firstly from the spiritual point of view. The spirit man has to overrule the soulish life and the earthy suit, which is our body.

The life of victory is the life of the spirit. the life of spirit is the life of the truth.

For the law of the Spirit of life in Christ Jesus hath made me free from the law of sin and death.

Romans 8:2.

There is no condemnation to those who walk in spirit, who walks according to the truth and righteous of God. The life of Christ is in his blood. When we have the blood of Jesus, we have the light of God. The works of the light always win.

From the scripture above, we know that if there is the law of spirit, then, there is the law of the flesh. The law of the spirit leads to life and the law of the flesh leads to death. We all know this.

It is pretty clear that to defeat the flesh, we ought to adhere to the law of the spirit. this is the life that is in Jesus Christ. On our own, we cannot defeat the power that comes from sexual lust, pornography, fornication, all kinds of pervasions, etc.

These things, sexual lust, masturbation, pornography, and fornication, are spirits. In the spirit realm, there is a demon called lust, a demon called porno, a demon called masturbation, and so on. As I have said, you cannot go to a warzone without weapons. You can only spiritually fight spirits. We fight the good fight of faith. And we know that we are dealing with spiritual wickedness in the air, these are princes of the power of the air.

If your approach has been fought from the ground level, your approach has to change. We are fighting the system that has been placed by the fallen angels. These are principalities that have billions of demons' spirits under their rule. The job description of every demon is to attack, harass, and torment until they destroy your destiny.

If you are the child of the light, your villain is children of darkness. Many are tormented in their sleep, strangled, and raped by demons. This is a living reality. And it doesn't mean they are not following God. Some are fighting the demons their forefathers fought. Some are living in torment and fear—experiencing the demons their forefathers bowed to.

Many things fall because of idol worship. If witchcraft, necromancy, and sorcery were part of your ancestral lineage, you are bound to suffer the consequences of marine power controlling your life, even your sexual life through dreams.

I have met many brothers and sisters in the Lord, who are staunch believers but experience strange things in their walking life and dream life. Knowing the roots, and the foundation of where you come from is vital for your deliverance.

This is a deliverance book birthed out of pain—seeing many even thinking of taking their life due to a strange spiritual covenant that they know nothing about. As you will dip into the knowledge of this book, I would like you to seriously partake in warfare prayers of deliverance at the end of this book for your redemption.

Also, as I have said, we win the victory of many things in life by adhering to the life of spirit, not the life of flesh. By reaching the point where we will say "It is no longer I who live but Christ in me", it is a roadmap to a triumphant life. Holiness is the greatest weapon that I know, in this life, and life to come.

What is sexual lust?

According to Google, sexual lust is a desire to engage in sexual activity. Sexual attraction is natural. Lust involves a choice and an act of will. A man or a woman can learn to overcome lust as he or she commits to self-control under the direct leadership of the Holy Spirit.

I had to explain what is sexual lust before we continue. Here, we are going to look at things from a spiritual point of view. From a spiritual point of view, lust is a spirit. That is why you need the Holy Spirit of God to defeat it. Under the umbrella of the Holy Spirit, there is the spirit of self-control.

Self-control preserves us. Satan, the prince of this world, fans the flames of the lust in the hearts of men and women. Playing on one of the strongest urges in nature—one that when controlled, is one of God's greatest gifts to mankind. The enemy throughout the ages, has perverted and brought destruction upon the victim through the power of lust, thus we say, sexual lust is spiritual.

Sex obsession is at an all-time high. Media feed us sex. Books, magazines, television, films, social media, etc. The demon of this end-time game has studied the patterns of humans, our deepest desires, likes, and dislikes, thus, the enemy will give you what you desire.

Pornography and masturbation start as the slightest thing, the more you feed on that energy, the more that energy will overrule your mind. It all start in the mind. The battle is in your mind as the enemy is after your mind. Mind is the aspect of your soul, likewise your emotions and your will. God has given a man a free will. However, there are some journeys that lead to darkness than light.

Sexual demons?

many believers do not believe in things like spirit spouses. While Apostle Paul got the letters, and teachings—half of the New Testament through personal revelation from the Holy Spirit, the Holy Spirit is still at work even today to reveal what need to be known. He is the reveler of hidden knowledge and secrets of the of the Lord.

The enemy, the Devil, works in ignorance. If you are ignorant to a certain doctrine, he will attack you more on that issue. If there is a whole in the bucket, the water cannot be filled to its proportion.

Knowledge is power!

1.Incubus and Succubus

Females – incubus (Latin – to lie upon)

Males – succubus (Latin – to lie under)

These spirits are spirits that seek to have sexual intercourse with men and women during the night hours. Incubus is described as a spirit being that comes to have intimate relationships with women while they are asleep while Succubus is described as a spirit being that comes to have relationships with men in their sleep. These dream visitors are called spirit husbands and spirit wives.

2. The demon Mare (nightmare) works with these spirits, causing dreams of sexual content. (It can manifest as a unicorn – a horse with a horn on the forehead). The demon MARE: Works with the Incubus and Succubus demons. The dream itself is called a nightmare. MARE: The supposed demon which, during the night, sits on the chest and causes feelings of suffocation and choking. Causing a feeling of being paralyzed and that the weight is crushing the breath out of a person. A similar sensation is associated with alien abductions

3. Asmodee (Asmodee is heavily involved with sexual immorality and responsible for the spirit of Jezebel & Lilith)

Those who associated with him in the past often call this power The Stinker. His appearance is that of a fat and smelly demonic-looking "man". He is tall and walks very lightly with a spring in his step. He also possesses wings similar to those of Beelzebub.

Asmodee is heavily involved with sexual immorality and he marries people for Satan. He is responsible for the spirit of Jezebel in the Bible and often works with Baal. 1 Kings 16:30-33

You can also see in 1 Kings 18 how the prophets of God were attacked through this Power. The Bible has much to say about the Jezebel spirit here and in Revelation. Asmodee works primarily with the Principality of Abaddon and reports to him.

The following problems in your life probably indicate the work of Asmodee:

1. Prostitution
2. Sexual perversion such as homosexuality, lesbianism, bestiality
3. Barrenness of the womb
4. Contempt for one's spouse and marital conflict
5. Repeated divorces and the inability to form permanent, cohesive relationships of the deepest kinds such as marriage.
6. Miscarriage and the death of children.

The primary responsibility of Asmodee is to pollute the human race with immorality. Because of this goal, he works with the other Principalities and Powers to foster sexual immorality, perversion, pornography, and prostitution. He marries people spiritually for Satan and has sex with them as do Satan and others. He is the demon responsible for spirit husbands and wives.

The head of all water spirits, Marine, is half women and half fish. She is where the image of a mermaid came from. Another ruler of the water spirit is Leviathan. This is the same Leviathan who started the original rebellion with Belial. He is found in Job 41, Ps. 74, and Is. 27:1.

In Christian marriage, Asmodee is interested in breaking down the morals of one or both partners. He is responsible for jealousy and uses it as a tool to promote adultery within the marriage. He is at work in many ways to destroy the holiness with which God created the institution of marriage. He is responsible for men who become "middle age crazy," leaving their wives and family for younger women. They find out to late, after the new relationship fades, that it was a mistake. He will also encourage a partner to just leave.

Asmodee encourages homosexuality as another means to destroy the institution of marriage. Today we see him actively at work encouraging society to do away with marriage altogether.

Asmodee gives to his partners the gifts of intelligence, beauty, and wealth (sometimes). They particularly like to obtain young women whom they send to the church to encourage sexual sins among the ministers. And she will find herself unable to be satisfied sexually by either a man or a woman (what we term nymphomania). This person's sex drive and function are totally out of control, being controlled and used by demons. If not delivered, she will eventually commit suicide.

As I think you can see, Asmodee is the Power most responsible for the destruction of the family as we know it today. He and Satan know that without the safety and security of the family unit, mankind is doomed. Because of his mission, he vehemently fights those organizations that are trying to save the family. He knows if he can stop the family, he can stop the work of God on the earth.

4.Lilith, Delilah, and Jezebel: Corrupting Influences in History and Mythology

Lilith

Lilith is a figure whose origins can be traced back to ancient Mesopotamian mythology. Over time, she has been incorporated into Jewish folklore and mysticism. In Jewish mythology, Lilith is often portrayed as Adam's first wife, who was created equally with him but left the Garden of Eden because she refused to submit to him. This narrative is not found in the canonical texts of the Bible but in later Jewish writings such as the Alphabet of Ben-Sira.

1. **Mythological Background**: In Mesopotamian mythology, Lilith was a demon or wind spirit associated with storms and desolation. In Jewish folklore, she evolved into a night demon who preys on pregnant women and infants, embodying sexual promiscuity and rebellion against patriarchal structures.

2. **Corrupting Influence**: Lilith's portrayal as a sexually liberated and rebellious figure has had a lasting impact on cultural depictions of female independence and sexuality. Her myth perpetuates the idea of a dangerous, seductive woman who uses her sexuality to corrupt men and society. This archetype has been used to demonize women who do not conform to traditional gender roles, suggesting that female independence and sexual freedom are inherently corrupting.

Delilah

Delilah is a well-known biblical figure from the Book of Judges, specifically in the story of Samson (Judges 16). She was a Philistine woman who was bribed by the lords of the Philistines to discover the secret of Samson's strength, which lay in his uncut hair.

1. **Biblical Background**: Delilah's betrayal of Samson is one of the most famous stories of seduction and deceit in the Bible.

She repeatedly coaxed Samson into revealing the source of his strength, ultimately leading to his capture and downfall when she cut his hair.

2. **Corrupting Influence**: Delilah represents the dangers of sexual manipulation and betrayal. Her story illustrates how sexual allure can be used to deceive and destroy. This narrative has been used throughout history to warn against the seductive power of women, reinforcing the idea that women's sexuality is a weapon that can lead men astray and cause societal downfall.

Jezebel

Jezebel is another prominent biblical figure, known for her role as a queen of Israel and the wife of King Ahab. Her story is primarily found in the Books of Kings (1 Kings 16:31; 2 Kings 9:30-37).

1. **Biblical Background**: Jezebel was a Phoenician princess who married Ahab, the king of Israel. She is infamous for promoting the worship of Baal and Asherah, leading Israel into idolatry and moral corruption. Jezebel was also known for her ruthless tactics, including the persecution of God's prophets and the orchestration of false charges against Naboth to seize his vineyard.

2. **Corrupting Influence**: Jezebel's name has become synonymous with seduction, idolatry, and moral corruption. Her influence in leading Israel away from God and into idolatry highlights the destructive power of manipulative and idolatrous leadership. The "spirit of Jezebel" is often cited in Christian circles as a demonic influence that promotes immorality, manipulation, and rebellion against God.

The Impact of These Archetypes on the World

The stories and mythologies surrounding Lilith, Delilah, and Jezebel have had a profound impact on cultural and religious perceptions of women and sexuality. These figures are often invoked as archetypes of sexual immorality and corruption, shaping societal attitudes in significant ways.

1. **Demonization of Female Sexuality**: These stories contribute to the demonization of female sexuality, portraying it as a dangerous and corrupting force. Women who exhibit sexual freedom or independence are often labeled with these archetypes, reinforcing negative stereotypes and gender biases.

2. **Moral and Spiritual Corruption**: The narratives of Lilith, Delilah, and Jezebel emphasize the potential for moral and spiritual corruption through sexual immorality and idolatry. They serve as cautionary tales warning against the dangers of turning away from God and succumbing to the temptations of the flesh.

3. **Influence on Modern Culture**: These archetypes continue to influence modern culture, from literature and media to religious teachings. The fear of female sexuality and power can be seen in various societal norms and practices that seek to control and suppress women's roles and rights.

How Believers Can Resist These Influences

1. **Biblical Understanding**: Educate oneself with a sound understanding of the Bible and its teachings on sexuality and relationships. Recognize that God's design for sexuality is within the bounds of marriage and that purity and holiness are central to Christian living.

2. **Personal Accountability**: Cultivate accountability in personal relationships. Share struggles and seek support from trusted friends, mentors, or spiritual leaders who can provide guidance

and prayer.

3. **Guarding the Heart and Mind**: Proverbs 4:23 advises, "Above all else, guard your heart, for everything you do flows from it." Be mindful of the media consumed, the company kept, and the thoughts entertained. Avoid content and situations that might lead to temptation.

4. **Spiritual Disciplines**: Engage in regular spiritual disciplines such as prayer, fasting, Bible study, and worship. These practices strengthen the spirit and help resist the lure of sinful desires.

5. **Seek Deliverance and Healing**: If struggling with the influences of these "spirits" or behaviors, seek deliverance through prayer and possibly the help of a deliverance minister. Healing and freedom are available through the power of Jesus Christ.

By understanding the historical and cultural impact of figures like Lilith, Delilah, and Jezebel, and actively seeking to align one's life with biblical principles, believers can resist the corrupting influences of sexual immorality and live in the freedom and purity that God desires.

Spiritual impurity?

When you are spiritually impure, it means your foot is on the door of Jesus and the other foot is on the door of Satan. Our ancestors were defeated the majority of them because of idol worship. What you worship owns you. When you worship God, He lead you, inspire you and direct you by his Holy Spirit. Likewise, when you obey the strange voice of the enemy of the gospel, he will lead you unconsciously to do things that are contrary to the will of God.

Purity is the call of God. Holiness is the aspect of God. We ought to be Holy as He is. A certain scripture says "Without holiness, we cannot see the face of God". It means we will not be fit to be in the presence of God. The atmosphere of the glory of God would not allow you to be among the just.

In this day and age, it's rare for people to allow someone who is physically dirty and smelly around them. Imagine if you are spiritually dirty. Is there any remedy for spiritual impurity? Yes, the answer is Christ. The blood of Christ is a serious weapon of purification. Not only purification but redemption as well. We need Jesus. The world needs Jesus. Salvation without Jesus is incomplete.

The law of flesh and sin leads to death. The law of spirit in Christ is the life of victory. The enemy, Satan, has millions of strategies to take us down that if it wasn't for the spirit of God indwelling us, we would have been defeated long ago.

It is not like we are honoring him but he has power. Fallen spirits have power over you if you are not fully surrender to the will of God. You cannot be saying the Devil is a liar while you are still fornicating as Christian.

It is a game of law in the spirit realm, the war is with words, but apart from words, your righteousness and holiness speaks louder. The gospel of old it was all about holiness and godly character, and adhering to the call of God. Christ was magnified. Christ was esteemed. Christ reigned in the hearts of men and women.

Now we are in the age of the coming of Anti-Christ. There are many brothers and sisters walking in the spirit of anti-Christ—denying the power of Christ and the kingship of Christ. However, adhering to the traditions of men and women that does not have anything to do with God.

When men and women bet way with God, all kinds of spirit that have left them will return seven times stronger than before. Thus, idol worship is one of those disease that lead to spiritual impurity. Out of idol worship comes all sorts of sins. When you break one law of Moses, you broke all.

The call of holiness is the call for all. The biggest investment one can make is to flee from sexual immorality. This is the biggest fiery dart coming out of the kingdom of darkness. As men or women, if the Devil can make you loose, it would take the grace and the mercy of God to bring out.

We can learn a lot from Joseph. We can also learn a lot from David. Men and women fall because of sexual ties outside the will of God. The will of God is sex within the institute of marriage.

Joseph fled from sexual immorality. In the day and age, we live in, you will be persecuted for fleeing immorality. Immorality is celebrated. Black is while, white is black. Unrighteousness is upholded, righteousness is condemned. It is all works of the enemy. The media space's propaganda is what sells. And if sex sells, it would be pushed until Jesus come.

Guard yourself in the Lord—purifies yourself in the blood of the lamb—building the capacity of spiritual atmosphere of praise and worship in your respected homes. The start in the family before he goes after the whole nation. Be like Abraham who departed from idol worship of his father's house. Joshua once said "I and my household we shall serve only the Lord".

What Constitutes Mental Impurity?

Mental impurity encompasses thoughts and fantasies that are contrary to God's standards of purity and holiness.

This includes:

1. **Fornication**: Mentally engaging in sexual fantasies or desires about engaging in premarital sex.
2. **Pornography**: Consuming and dwelling on sexually explicit images, videos, or written material that objectify and degrade human sexuality.
3. **Adultery**: Entertaining thoughts of infidelity, longing for or imagining sexual encounters with someone other than one's spouse.
4. **Lust**: Harboring intense or uncontrolled sexual desires for someone, reducing them to mere objects of gratification.

Effects on the Conscious and Subconscious Mind

1. **Conscious Mind**: The conscious mind is actively aware of thoughts and decisions. When one engages in mentally impure thoughts, the immediate effects include feelings of guilt, shame, and spiritual disconnect from God. It leads to a weakened resolve to live a holy life and often manifests in external behaviors that reflect inner turmoil.

It is the feeling of dirty or worthless after engaging in sexual activity outside the will of God. Your spiritual man convicts you, for it is the carrier of the glory of God. The Holy Spirit of God is intertwined with the spirit man, thus, when you are on something contrary to the likeness of God, it disapproves you.

We all ought to listen to our intuition, everyone of us has that small still voice in their heart that speaks to them from time to time.

1. **Subconscious Mind**: The subconscious mind stores and processes information below the level of conscious awareness. Repeated exposure to and engagement in mentally impure thoughts embed these images and desires deep within the subconscious, influencing attitudes, emotions, and behaviors over time. This can lead to increased temptation, compulsive behavior, and difficulty maintaining pure thoughts even when consciously trying to do so.

I am pretty sure that it has happen to you that when you listen to a certain type of music, you can even hear that music in your sleep from afar. It is as if you are listen to music coming from afar distance. It just basically playing in your mind—your subconscious mind keeps the record of everything it was exposed to earlier.

Let's say you are watching a horror movie, in most cases in your sleep the flashing imagines will be in display. Things like pornography or over sexualized music, robs us our identity of who we are in Christ. The subconscious mind is the spiritual eye of our mind. We can do a good job as believers by memorizing scriptures since the subconscious mind stores information. Walking in spirit means feeding your spirit and soul with spiritual food.

How Mental Impurity Affects Us

1. **Spiritual Health**: Mental impurity separates us from God, as sin creates a barrier between us and our Creator. It hinders our

ability to hear God's voice and diminishes our desire to pursue Him fully.

It is innate every one's soul to want to hear from God. Dreams and visions are the ways mostly God reaches us. A mind filled with the things of this world wouldn't be able to discern the voice of the Holy Spirit. a faith filled believer with the Word of God in his heart will always thrive in this generation packed with distraction.

We can all see that the enemy is distracting us technology at our disposal. With just a smart phone, you have the whole world in the palm of your hand. While we cannot shy away from it, we can use it for the benefit of the kingdom of God.

1. **Emotional Well-being**: Engaging in mentally impure thoughts often leads to emotional instability. Guilt and shame can cause anxiety, depression, and a sense of worthlessness, affecting overall mental health.

Through my research, I have noted that many people who come out of addictions such as musterbation, pornography, or any other type, feels a sense of worthless. It is like Adam and Eve after they committed the first sense, they fled from the face of God. Any man and women can attest to this feeling; remorse, guilt and shame.

The soul compasses of the mind, will and emotion. It is the soul that is affected. And when the soul is weakened, the whole body become sick. The legs we stand on is the legs of the Holy Spirit. allow the spirit of the Living God to transform you into the very best image of the Living God. Victory is in Christ, who was tempted in all but conquered all, even death itself.

Remember that, it was the spirit of God that raised Christ from the dead, He will also quicken our weakness if we allow Him. If we abide not in our weakness but in His shadow of grace and mercy.

1. **Relational Health**: Mental impurity can damage relationships. Lustful thoughts and fantasies can lead to unrealistic expectations of partners, decrease emotional intimacy, and contribute to infidelity and broken trust in relationships.

Avoiding Mental Impurity Through the Word of God

1. **Renewing the Mind**: Romans 12:2 instructs us to be transformed by the renewing of our minds. Regular meditation on Scripture helps replace impure thoughts with godly ones.

Philippians 4:8 encourages believers to think about things that are true, noble, right, pure, lovely, and admirable. Consistently focusing on these virtues renews our minds and aligns our thoughts with God's standards.

When you think positive, you will automatically live positively. It is written that "As He thinketh, so is he". Right thinking can change your mood, or emotions. Also, being around believers or people in general who uplifts you will change how you look at yourself. As Christ is he, so are we in this world.

1. **Hiding God's Word in Our Hearts**: Psalm 119:11 says, "I have hidden your word in my heart that I might not sin against you."

Memorizing and meditating on Scripture equips us to combat impure thoughts. When tempted, recalling relevant verses provides strength and guidance to resist.

We do not talk about dreams and visions a lot, and we spend most if not half of our lives sleeping. Therefore, the word in is will also affects our dream life. The Word is powerful, the word is prophetic. When the word of Christ is hidden in your, your spirit and soul become transformed into the image of His being. Our greatest calling is to be transformed to his image. To be Holy and pure, as He is.

The power is in His Word. Here is what David had to say about the Word of God.

Psalm 138:2 I will worship toward thy holy temple, and praise thy name for thy
lovingkindness and for thy truth: for thou hast magnified thy word above all thy
name.

1. **Guarding Our Minds**: Proverbs 4:23 advises us to guard our hearts, as everything we do flows from it. This includes being mindful of what we expose ourselves to. Avoiding movies, music, websites, and literature that promote impurity is crucial. Setting boundaries and using accountability software can help maintain purity in our media consumption.
2. **Prayer and Dependence on the Holy Spirit**: Prayer is essential in maintaining mental purity. Asking God for strength, wisdom, and purity of mind helps us stay vigilant against temptation. Galatians 5:16 encourages us to "walk by the Spirit, and you will not gratify the desires of the flesh." Dependence on the Holy Spirit empowers us to live a life that honors God.

3. **Accountability and Community**: Ecclesiastes 4:9-10 emphasizes the strength found in community. Having accountability partners or joining small groups provides support, encouragement, and prayer in the journey towards mental purity. Confessing struggles to trusted friends and mentors' fosters transparency and mutual edification.

4. **Filling the Mind with Godly Content**: Replace time spent on potentially impure content with godly alternatives. Engage in reading the Bible, Christian literature, listening to worship music, and watching edifying Christian media. This not only distracts from temptation but fills the mind with God-honoring thoughts.

5. **Fasting and Spiritual Discipline**: Fasting helps break the power of fleshly desires and brings clarity and focus on spiritual matters. It's a powerful discipline that can aid in overcoming mental impurity. Combining fasting with prayer and meditation on Scripture intensifies the transformative process.

Practical Steps

1. **Daily Devotion**: Set aside time each day for Bible study and prayer. Make it a priority to start and end your day with God's Word. David was a man after God's heart because he praised and worshipped the Lord no matter the circumstance. He was the living altar of worship and praise, that, he composed so many prophetic Psalms, Hymns and Songs.

2. **Scripture Memorization**: Regularly memorize verses that address purity and temptation. This equips you with a spiritual arsenal to combat impure thoughts.

some believers keep the repeating a certain scripture over and over again till the scripture became ingrain in their mind. While some speak forth the scripture, these are all part of scripture meditation and memorization.

The people of Moses were told to keep the word near them. The Word near you will be a banner of a refuge when in need. There are different seasons in life—in the wilderness season, you are going to need all the arsenal to make it through.

Usually, I sing the Word, this is part of my scripture meditation and memorization. You can literally sing your own songs unto the Lord. The Psalmist always say "Sing unto the Lord a new song". Glorify, honor, praise, and worship the king with a sincere heart.

1. **Monitor Media Intake**: Be proactive in choosing what to watch, listen to, and read. Use filters and accountability tools to guard against explicit content. This is so important since we are exposed to a lot of things, especially through our phones, and lusts start through the eyes.

The spiritual portals of your body is your eyes, ears, mouth, hands and feet. These are the portal which spirit get through. Some of you maybe surprise by the hands and feet. What you walk on, and what you touch, if it is not under the spirit of God, can affect you. Spirit of witchcraft get through the hands and feet.

However, spirit of lust is through the eyes. What you see is what you get. It is the lust of the eye, the lust of the flesh and the pride of life. Men and women can become the conquer through Christ. Without Christ, we are fallen beings.

1. **Seek God's Guidance**: Continually ask God for help in maintaining purity. Praying for a pure heart and mind should be a constant request. Above all, talk to the man of God you trust about your issues. There is always light at the end of the tunnel. Light arises in the darkness. God in the beginning divided light from the darkness. The power is in the light since the Almighty One said "Let there be light".

2. **Engage in Fellowship**: Surround yourself with a community of believers who encourage and support your commitment to purity. It always come to this "Two is better than one".

By understanding the profound impact of mental impurity and actively seeking to align our thoughts with God's Word, believers can cultivate a pure mind that honors God and fosters spiritual growth. This ongoing process of sanctification is essential for living a life that reflects the holiness of Christ.

Secret thoughts.

Deliverance from the Lord touches every aspect of self. I always wondered why my thoughts processes weren't displaying the true character of a believer. When your negative thoughts overshadow your positive thoughts, right there, that's the problem.

As we are delivered from spirits, we also should not neglect the mental aspects of our being. The spirit of God should supersede our negative emotions, negative feelings, and negative mindset.

Through my experience and through the Word of God, I have learned that if your life is ruled by how your mental state is, you will leave a life of defeat—a roller-coaster life that does not paint the good picture of a Christian lifestyle. Mental state fluctuates. Men and women changes. Only God is the same yesterday, today and forever.

Emotions are red and blue. But the faith in God is power, since it is not ruled by emotions or feelings. Men and women who reaches to the point where it is no longer them that live but Christ, are able to maneuver through in this life, and become conquerors.

Secrets thoughts are those we harbor of lust, sexual desires and appetite through unfulfilled desires. Some it many just be pure lusts. And these develop till they become stronghold in the life of a person. The enemy will only target your weakest spot till it gets to the point where you cannot control your sexual obsessions and desires.

Sex outside marriage is a connection of spirit, soul and body to another person whom you will end up no marrying. Sex is spiritual. It is sacred to God. That is why Paul says the marriage bed should not be defiled.

Paul say whatever that is pure, holy and true, we should think of those. Meaning, we have to think about who we are in Christ. Christ is seated in the heavenly places. We are also seated with him spiritual since when He rose, He raised us up with Him in the heavenly places far above principalities and powers. Christ fills the whole heavens. He in the third heaven. Above domains, kingdoms, and thrones that we see with our eyes, and that we do not see with our naked eyes.

A changed of thoughts is power when it comes to taming the power of the flesh; sexual lusts, homosexuality, adultery, or fornication. The Word of God is able to transform and renew your mind to the will of God.

It is in our power since authority is bestowed upon us to demolish strongholds and to cast down evil imaginations. Everything in your mind that does not alight with the character of Christ has to go.

3 For though we walk in the flesh, we do not war after the flesh:
4 (For the weapons of our warfare are not carnal, but mighty through God
to
the pulling down of strong holds;)
5 Casting down imaginations, and every high thing that exalteth itself
against the knowledge of God, and bringing into captivity every thought to
the
obedience of Christ;
2 Corinthians 10:3.

The truth is that through the mighty weapons of God, we can do valiant things. On our own we can do nothing. God takes us as warriors and soldiers. The term used throughout Paul's writing is a military term. When the children of Israel came out of the land of Egypt, God called them His army.

Whether you are strong or weak, you are one of the army of the Lord. What does army do? The army defend for their country through warfare. From time to time they engage in warfare—whether defensive or offensive. Throughout your faith journey, you will also have to fight your own battles and the battles of your family.

We are fighting for territories in spirit. when you are defeated, it means the enemy will infiltrate your land. That's what the Devils do, he wants to rule and control your home. But firstly he has to influence your mind, eventually, he will have a total control. He is after the mind. We should not allow this as the army of the Lord. We have to stand strong in the Lord. The battle is for the Lord, however, He uses us on this earth to accomplish His tasks.

The kingdom of the air and the fall of Lucifer.

I don't know how many times my spirit went to the kingdom of the air. I have had out-of-body experiences, visions, and dreams about the kingdom of the air. The kingdom that Apostle Paul wrote about in Ephesians 6:12.

It is a kingdom, but a spiritual one—ruled by the prince of the air. The Devil is called the prince of the power of the air. You cannot dodge his influence if you are not in CHRIST. You have to be a serious and zealous believer if you are to be a warrior and a conqueror, and a student of the Word and spirit to defeat the powers of evil.

I have written articles, books, and eBooks explaining about the three heavens. The second heaven theory is not scriptural, however, as Apostle Paul was caught up in the Third heaven, in Paradise, logically we can assume that there is the first, second, and third. Some things we are going to need the person of the HOLY SPIRIT to reveal them to us.

The LORD GOD has been gracious to us by manifesting Himself unto us through dreams, visions, angels, through His word, and other means of communication. We cannot box the LORD in a container. His ways cannot be comprehended. As heaven is far above the earth, so are His ways.

In the second heaven, there are spirits, human spirits that are bound, some people are still on this earth. Strange fallen beings are holding in hostage the souls of men and humans. And when the times come, or when they die, their soul are already captured in the spirit realm to work for the kingdom of darkness.

A soul that is not covered by the blood of the lamb is bound by the powers of the air. On your own, you cannot defeat the evil influence of Satan in your waking life. You need the WORD, HOLY SPIRIT, and THE BLOOD.

The Devil is a soul snatcher, he looks at your generational DNA, if there is an open door of any kind, he will throw arrows until he brings you down. One of the greatest ignorance I have witnessed in those people bound, mostly it was due to sexual immorality, fornication, or abortion. Not to say these are great sins, but there is no small sin—sin is a sin.

In these last days, sexual sins have skyrocketed. Many fall because of sexual contact before marriage.

Marriages have collapsed. Leaders have fallen. Preachers, pastors, and prophets have lost dignity. The enemy is playing the chess game here.

These are the realm that cages the souls of men; the marine kingdom under the sea, the second heaven, and the kingdom underground. We can also include the occultist, witches, and wizards who cages the souls of men and women through their demonic powers.

Let's talk about the air realm. There is the first heaven, the second heaven, and the third heaven. The disembodied spirits are the evil spirits of the Nephilim destroyed during the floods of Noah. Lucifer also fell with millions of angels. Apart from Lucifer, 200 watchers had sex with women—recorded in the book of Enoch and Genesis 6. The evil spirits hover around in the sky, looking for a way to a man. The sin of man gives this spirit legal authority to enter man's body.

It is to say, above our homes, in the air, there a thousands of evil spirits. Above the peak of the mountain, in the space of the clouds, there is a strongman who gives orders to these demons. Strongman is a serious power of authority. There are levels of degrees in the demonic. JESUS CHRIST granted us the power to cast out demons and also to bind strongmen.

The first heaven is where the powers of authority seats. They control what is going on in a region. But they have control only where they have legal rights. Satan can only control where there is a legal right to do so. He is limited.

The second heaven is his domain—headquarters. Where there are dangerous spirits like the queen of heaven, Ashtoreth, Jezebel, etc. this is the kingdom like any other kingdom. This is where the souls of men and women are caged. The real battle of spiritual warfare is here but with the angelic beings. This is where Angel Michael fought the Prince of Persia for the release of Gabriel to bring Daniel's message.

Principalities mostly name themselves according to the city of the domain they rule. If there was a principality in Johannesburg, he would call himself the prince of Johannesburg. However, these are fallen angels. You cannot cast them out. They are not demons but fallen angels. You can only restrict their assignment. You can be like Daniel and intercede for the dispatcher of angelic powers like Michael to fight for you when dealing with serious powers.

If you can picture yourself seated in the heavenly places with CHRIST, your faith will explode. Your level of spiritual perception will change. You start seeing yourself as above principalities and powers of darkness as you are seated in the seat of authority with CHRIST who has triumphed.

Colossians 1:15 Who is the image of the invisible God, the firstborn of every creature:
16 For by him were all things created, that are in heaven, and that are in earth, visible and invisible, whether they be thrones, or dominions, or principalities, or powers: all things were created by him, and for him: 17 And he is before all things, and by him all things consist.

We are dealing with the invisible kingdoms that are pulling strings in the background. The naked eye cannot see spirits. Through the eyes of your mind—the Holy Spirit, you can see beyond time and space.

This few months I have been researching and writing about the discerning spirit (Spirit of discernment). This gift is important especially when dealing with spiritual attacks from the realm of darkness. It comes with words of wisdom, knowledge, and understanding of the spirit world.

Many times my life has been spared through this gift. And many has ago, I had a personal encounter with the LORD, and He was telling me about "intuition". Sometimes you will not get the word for a specific thing, or rather prophecy for a season when you need it most, if you can follow your intuition—your spirit within, you will succeed because the Holy Spirit is intertwined with our spirit, and bear witness to your heart.

This is also important when you are dealing with the marine powers. You will need the word for the moment. Your dream and vision life has to be covered by the power of the BLOOD OF JESUS. Marine powers works through dreams and visions. Sometimes they will confuse your life. Cover everything with the blood of the Cross. The power of GOD shall be revealed. Sing Holy Spirit-inspired songs—especially about the power of the BLOOD OF CHRIST.

Ephesians 1:19 And what is the exceeding greatness of his power to us-
ward who
believe, according to the working of his mighty power,
20 Which he wrought in Christ, when he raised him from the dead, and
set
him at his own right hand in the heavenly places,

CHRIST's priesthood is different from others, His priesthood is eternal. This means that you have been with CHRIST all along before you were even created, spiritually. The kingdom of GOD is spiritual. GOD is spiritual. JESUS CHRIST is a spirit being. However, He came in the bodily form for our redemption. The redemption plan of GOD has been ever since before creation. GOD knows the end from the beginning. Knows the thoughts of a man from afar.

In spirit, you are crafted in CHRIST who overcame. And that makes you an overcomer! Even though darkness has its way around us, we are the light of this world through CHRIST. Stir up your light! Arise and shine!

Ephesians 1:21 Far above all principality, and power, and might, and dominion, and

minion, and

every name that is named, not only in this world, but also in that which is

to

come:

In the world to come CHRIST is still the KINGS! The wisdom of this world would try to convince you that Satan does not exist; it is all in your mind. The people in high power are those blinding many to believe the fallacy. Our enemy, the Devil sits at the seat of high authority in this world—manipulating, controlling, stealing, and killing.

A defeated foe indeed! But the media magnifies him to weaken man's faith. Our gateway through the presence of GOD is the Holy Spirit. the Holy Spirit in you is bigger than Satan a million times. The Holy Spirit is GOD. In other words, GOD resides in you. CHRIST in you is the hope of your glory. CHRIST in you is your salvation. No weapon formed against us shall prosper. It is the truth that shall set people free. In the name of the LORD GOD MOST HIGH be free!

GOD is above culture. GOD is above religion. GOD is above tradition. GOD is above all wisdom, all knowledge, and all understanding. Serve Him only in the name of JESUS CHRIST!

Ephesians 2:6 And hath raised us up together, and made us sit together in heavenly

places in Christ Jesus:

As we are in CHRIST, we have all the spiritual blessings to free ourselves and our brethren from spiritual bondage of all kinds. The Psalmist says we are a little lower than the angels. This is great authority indeed. What's more? Psalm 82:6 *"Ye are gods"*. We all come from the HOLY ONE!

Psalm 82:6 I have said, Ye are gods; and all of you are children of the most High.

In dealing with the demonic realm like the marine kingdom, a very basic strategy of success in war is to know one's enemy. Without exception, a general would never take his army against another army without first preparing the soldiers.

Foundational to that preparation would be a study of the strengths and weaknesses of the enemy. Failure to study the enemy would virtually guarantee defeat— even if the opposing army were inferior. Throughout this book, I talk in depth about who our enemy is, you will be surprised that even though this book is about the marine battle, most focus is on the Devil himself and overcoming strategies of victory against his tricks.

Most of my writing is in line of spiritual warfare and prayer mainly because we are in war. The battle is for the LORD but He uses us as His mighty army to dismantle the powers of darkness throughout the world. People must be free from demonic entanglement. There is freedom in the LORD.

CHRIST has to be known from sun rising to sun down. This is the greatest commission of the gospel.

Psalm 34: 8 O taste and see that the LORD is good: blessed is the man that trusteth in

him.

Marine kingdom cages.

We have already talked about the second heaven territory. We as the body of CHRIST are endowed from above by the MOST HIGH in CHRIST. We are seated in the heavenly places spiritually. We fight from a heavenly perspective. And we fight the good fight of faith.

Marine cages are prison cells where they keep the souls of men and women. The kingdom under the sea is responsible for many atrocious activities happening in the world and in the body of CHRIST.

CHRIST is raising the generation of believers who will not only be limited by time and space, but wherever the spirit leads them, they will go. As Philip was time traveling through the spirit of GOD, his end-time armies shall work the kingdom business in the spirit realm, taking territories and demolishing the works of the Evil one. In the spirit, the realm is about power and authority. It is about territories and the powers of the Words.

The kingdom of CHRIST is the kingdom of power demonstrated by the words of power through the HOLY SPIRIT. When you have the Word and spirit of CHRIST, you can shake the nations.

Sadly, many do have them but practice only one. Many read the Word staunchly, however, fail to invite the person of the HOLY SPIRIT to take over. In the beginning, GOD spoke and commanded, and it was established, the heavens and the earth. He spoke the Word, and the HOLY SPIRIT acted upon the Word. We are to speak the Word in every situation we may encounter, it is the HOLY SPIRIT that shall act upon the Word. Even in the ministry of Angels, angels act only upon the Word of GOD.

As CHRIST led the captivity after His death, we are to practice deliverance. Lead our friends and family out of the land of destruction. Out of the pit of hell. There are many spirits of the people on this earth that are in hell already while still living. I have seen many souls caged in the second heaven, under the sea, in the mountains, etc. By the way, mountains, and seas are portals to the other side of the world. Many rituals in this world are either done in the mountains or the seas.

As I write to you reader, you may be having friends and family members who are in bondage. We do not have to fear; CHRIST is the bondage breaker. The Devil is already defeated but he does not want you to know it. we already know that his kingdom is built upon fear, lies, manipulation, and deception. He rebelled to GOD. He wants you to rebel also.

In the next chapters, I will include a deliverance plan for freedom. And fire prayers which are scriptural to defeat the powers of hell. Do not allow hell to enlarge itself upon your life and your family. The recipe and the remedy is to fight the good fight of faith. Fight through righteousness. Fight through faith. Fight through peace. Fight through with all kinds of prayers. Sing in spirit like King David. Be mighty with the sword (Word of GOD) like Joshua. DELIVERANCE AND BLESSINGS COME FROM THE LORD (PSALM 3:9).

The Effects of Pornography, Masturbation, and Fornication and How Believers Can Avoid Them

The Effects of Pornography

Pornography has pervasive and detrimental effects on individuals, relationships, and society as a whole. Consuming pornographic content can lead to a host of psychological, emotional, and spiritual issues.

1. **Psychological Effects**: Pornography consumption can alter brain function, creating a dependency similar to drug addiction. It can lead to desensitization, where more extreme content is required to achieve the same level of arousal, which can escalate compulsive behavior.

Studies have shown that pornography can impair memory, reduce cognitive function, and decrease overall mental health, leading to anxiety and depression.

1. **Emotional Effects**: Pornography often creates unrealistic expectations about sex, body image, and relationships. This can lead to dissatisfaction with real-life partners and relationships, fostering feelings of inadequacy, insecurity, and loneliness. It can also cause emotional withdrawal and reduce the ability to form genuine emotional connections.
2. **Spiritual Effects**: For believers, consuming pornography is a sin that separates them from God. It distorts the sanctity of sex, which is meant to be a sacred union between husband and wife. Engaging in this behavior grieves the Holy Spirit and can hinder spiritual growth and intimacy with God.

The Effects of Masturbation

Masturbation, while often viewed as a natural behavior, can have negative consequences when it becomes compulsive or is accompanied by lustful thoughts and fantasies.

1. **Psychological Effects**: Masturbation can lead to guilt and shame, especially when it is in conflict with personal or religious beliefs. It can also become a coping mechanism for stress or loneliness, which prevents individuals from developing healthier ways to manage their emotions.

2. **Emotional Effects**: Excessive masturbation can create a reliance on self-gratification rather than seeking intimacy with others. This can lead to isolation and difficulties in forming or maintaining healthy relationships. It can also perpetuate feelings of loneliness and emptiness.

3. **Spiritual Effects**: Masturbation often involves lustful thoughts, which are condemned in the Bible. Jesus said in Matthew 5:28, "But I tell you that anyone who looks at a woman lustfully has already committed adultery with her in his heart." This behavior can be a barrier to spiritual purity and holiness, affecting one's relationship with God.

The Effects of Fornication

Fornication, or sexual intercourse outside of marriage, has serious consequences on multiple levels.

1. **Physical Effects**: Engaging in sexual activity outside of marriage increases the risk of sexually transmitted infections (STIs) and unplanned pregnancies. These physical consequences can have long-lasting impacts on health and well-being.

2. **Emotional Effects**: Fornication can lead to emotional trauma, especially if the relationship is casual or ends poorly. It can also

create bonds with multiple partners, making it difficult to form a stable, trusting, and lasting relationship in the future.

3. **Spiritual Effects**: Fornication is a sin that defiles the body, which is meant to be a temple of the Holy Spirit (1 Corinthians 6:18-20). This behavior is contrary to God's design for sexual intimacy within marriage and can lead to feelings of guilt, shame, and spiritual disconnection from God.

How Believers Can Avoid These Sins

Avoiding pornography, masturbation, and fornication requires intentional actions and reliance on God's strength. Here are practical steps believers can take:

1. **Cultivate a Strong Relationship with God**: Regular prayer, Bible study, and worship are essential for maintaining a close relationship with God. This relationship provides the spiritual strength needed to resist temptation.

2. **Renew Your Mind**: Romans 12:2 urges believers to be transformed by the renewing of their minds. Filling your mind with God's Word helps replace sinful thoughts with pure and holy ones. Meditate on scriptures like Philippians 4:8, which encourages us to think about things that are true, noble, right, pure, lovely, and admirable.

3. **Practice Accountability**: Having an accountability partner can provide support and encouragement. This person can pray with you, check in on your progress, and offer guidance and support during times of temptation.

4. **Set Boundaries**: Create and maintain boundaries to avoid situations where temptation is likely. This might include using internet filters to block pornographic content, avoiding situations that could lead to sexual temptation, and refraining from being alone with someone of the opposite sex in compromising settings.

5. **Engage in Healthy Activities**: Find fulfilling and productive activities to occupy your time and energy. Exercise, hobbies, volunteering, and spending time with family and friends can provide positive outlets and reduce the likelihood of falling into sinful behaviors.

6. **Seek Professional Help**: If you find yourself struggling to overcome these behaviors, consider seeking help from a Christian counselor or therapist. They can provide strategies and support to help you break free from these habits.

7. **Join a Support Group**: Many churches and Christian organizations offer support groups for those struggling with sexual sin. Being part of a community that understands your struggles and offers prayer and support can be incredibly beneficial.

8. **Stay Engaged in Church**: Regularly attending church services and participating in small groups or Bible studies can keep you grounded in your faith and provide a support network to help you stay strong in your commitment to purity.

By relying on God's power and applying these practical steps, believers can overcome the temptations of pornography, masturbation, and fornication. Living a life of purity not only honors God but also brings true peace, fulfillment, and spiritual growth.

The Effects of Sexual Content in Movies and Music

Sexual content in movies and music has become increasingly prevalent, often glorifying and normalizing behaviors that are contrary to biblical values. The consumption of such content can have profound effects on individuals, relationships, and society.

1. **Psychological Effects**: Exposure to sexual content in media can shape and distort viewers' perceptions of sex and relationships. It can lead to unrealistic expectations and the objectification of others. Research shows that repeated exposure to sexual content can desensitize individuals, making them more accepting of sexually explicit material and behaviors. This desensitization can also decrease sensitivity to the consequences of such behaviors.

2. **Emotional Effects**: Consuming sexual content can affect emotional well-being. It often fosters feelings of inadequacy and insecurity, as individuals compare themselves to the idealized and often exaggerated portrayals they see. This can lead to a negative self-image and low self-esteem, particularly in adolescents who are still forming their sense of identity.

3. **Relational Effects**: Sexual content can undermine healthy relationships. It promotes a casual attitude towards sex, which can erode the sanctity of marital intimacy. It can also contribute to infidelity and a lack of commitment in relationships, as it fosters a culture of instant gratification and disposability. The portrayal of sex without emotional or relational context can lead to shallow, unfulfilling relationships.

4. **Spiritual Effects**: For believers, indulging in sexually explicit media is a form of sin that grieves the Holy Spirit and hinders

spiritual growth. It diverts focus from God to fleshly desires, creating a barrier to a deeper relationship with Him. Jesus taught in Matthew 5:28 that even looking at someone lustfully is equivalent to committing adultery in the heart, highlighting the spiritual danger of consuming sexual content.

How We Can Avoid Sexual Content in Media

Avoiding sexual content in movies and music requires intentional effort and discipline. Here are practical steps believers can take to guard their hearts and minds:

1. **Be Selective with Media Choices**: Before watching a movie or listening to music, research its content. Websites and apps that provide detailed reviews and ratings can help you identify and avoid sexually explicit material. Opt for media that aligns with biblical values and promotes positive messages.

Apart from being selective, you have the Holy Spirit in you that is the director of the movie of your life. And other important gifting of the spirits such as the discerning of spirits—to discern between good and evil. Sometimes every evil door opened in our lives, it is merely our choices due to ignorance of the will of God, and His status.

1. **Set Personal Boundaries**: Establish clear boundaries for the types of media you consume. Decide in advance what content is acceptable and what is not. This might include setting limits on movie genres, avoiding certain artists, or steering clear of specific streaming platforms that frequently feature explicit content.
2. **Use Content Filters and Parental Controls**: Utilize available technology to filter out inappropriate content. Many streaming services, internet providers, and devices offer parental controls

and content filters that can block or restrict access to sexually explicit material.

3. **Create an Accountability System**: Having an accountability partner can help you stay committed to avoiding inappropriate content. Share your media boundaries with a trusted friend or mentor who can check in with you regularly and provide support and encouragement.

4. **Cultivate a Healthy Media Diet**: Replace sexually explicit media with wholesome alternatives. Seek out movies, music, and other forms of entertainment that are uplifting and edifying. Christian movies, family-friendly films, and music that glorifies God can provide positive, enriching entertainment.

5. **Engage in Spiritual Activities**: Fill your time with activities that strengthen your faith and draw you closer to God. Regular prayer, Bible study, worship, and serving in your community can help keep your focus on spiritual growth rather than worldly distractions.

6. **Be Mindful of Triggers**: Identify situations or emotions that trigger the desire to consume sexual content and develop strategies to address them. This might include finding healthy ways to cope with stress, loneliness, or boredom, such as exercising, pursuing hobbies, or spending time with loved ones.

7. **Educate Yourself and Others**: Learn about the impact of sexual content on the mind and spirit, and educate others, especially children and teenagers, about these dangers. Open conversations about media choices and their effects can foster a supportive environment where everyone is encouraged to make wise decisions.

8. **Seek God's Help**: Pray for strength and wisdom to resist the temptation of sexually explicit media. Ask God to help you guard your heart and mind and to provide discernment in your

media choices. Philippians 4:8 encourages believers to think about things that are true, noble, right, pure, lovely, and admirable, which can serve as a guide for media consumption.

9. **Replace Negative Influences with Positive Ones**: Surround yourself with influences that support your commitment to purity. This might include joining a Bible study group, following Christian content creators, or immersing yourself in worship music and faith-based podcasts.

By taking these proactive steps, believers can avoid the negative effects of sexual content in movies and music and maintain a lifestyle that honors God. Embracing media that uplifts and edifies not only protects the mind and spirit but also fosters a deeper, more fulfilling relationship with God and others.

God's intentions for sexual fulfilment lie strictly within the covenant of marriage. Marriage is not just a legal transaction. It is primarily a spiritual transaction - a joining together of two people. Just as men (and women) are spirit, soul and body, then God also intended the covenant of marriage to lead to a permanent union of spirit, soul and body.

A couple who intend to marry may be spiritually joined in faith, heart and intent, but until after the vows have been made to each other and to God, and intercourse has taken place, the marriage is not complete. Thus, sexual intercourse is the legal binding in this case. Intercourse is the union of flesh, when the desire of the soul is completed through bodily sexual union. Through sexual union, therefore, there is both a joining of spirit and soul and a joining of bodies.

After intercourse has taken place the bodies separate, but the souls are now joined together – the marriage, as such, is complete. There is then not only a union of spirit, but also a union of soul.

Scripture talks about the two having become one flesh (Ephesians 5:31). There is now a soul-tie established between husband and wife through the act of sexual union. Something of the man becomes part of the woman and something of the woman becomes part of the man.

What we have now established is that the physical union of sexual intercourse involves more than the physical joining of bodies, for those who have been joined together in this way also become joined together in their souls with what we call a soul-tie. This was God's wonderful plan for marriage, permanently uniting couples in a living and dynamic relationship.

Consequences of Sexual Sin

We have already established that when people enter into sexual sin, they are pleasing the god of this world and, as a result, they may have welcomed an unclean spirit into their lives for which deliverance is needed.

We have now understood that God's intention for marriage was to provide a means through which man and woman would be permanently united in spirit and soul. Paul even tells us that God's intentions for the relationship between husband and wife could even be used as a picture of God's intentions for the relationship between Jesus and the Church! (Ephesians 5). That's the good news!

The bad news for those who are sexually promiscuous is that God does not suspend his plans to establish a soul-tie between them in order to accommodate man's sin. Whilst God is undoubtedly a God of love, he is also a God of law and order and God's order for sexual relationships is that whenever they occur a joining takes place and a soul-tie is established.

So if a person, for example, had several sexual partners in their youth, he (or she) now has a soul-tie with each one of these. Something of themselves has been given away to each sexual partner and something of the other person has become part of them. Paul explicitly stated that this is even so in the case of prostitution, where he says that when a man unites himself with a prostitute "the two will become one flesh" (1 Cor. 6:16).

Instead of this being a Godly soul-tie which brings great blessing into the lives of a husband and wife, it becomes a chain of bondage through which people are influenced unknowingly by the life and personality of those to whom they have been sexually joined. And additionally an ungodly soul-tie provides an opportunity for the demonic to transfer from one person to another, both at the time of sexual intercourse and at any time subsequently.

The whole of Proverbs 5 is a warning against adulterous sexual relationships. Verse 22 sums up the consequences of ungodly sex by saying that "the evil deeds of a wicked man ensnare him; the cords of his sin hold him fast." An ungodly soul-tie is a cord of sin which holds people in permanent bondage – at least until Jesus breaks the chain. Because it is through God's order for mankind that a soul-tie was established in the first place, it follows that it is only God who can undo it.

Breaking the Chains of Ungodly Soul-Ties

1 John 1:9 encourages us to confess our sins to God so that we will be forgiven. But in James 5:16 scripture tells us to "confess your sins one to another, and pray for each other, so that you may be healed". True repentance is need when we embark on the journey of breaking soul ties. We will renounce and denounce the spiritual ties with have made with people we intermingled with sexually outside the will of God.

A perfect marriage happens when men and women comes clean to keep the marriage bed pure. Just imagine one partner comes with 10 souls and another partner comes with 10 souls—all tight to them. There would be able to connect to each other in spirit, soul and body, and that's where the deliverance comes in, the old is gone, the new has come.

We have to learn that spirituality governs the physical. Whatsoever that happen under the sun, it is the manifestation of the spiritual reality. So is your body, temple that carries the glory of God. If you share your glory with others, you will become powerless and defiled as well. Keep the marriage bed pure.

Many people suffer because they traded their glory with the kingdom of darkness. Not all men and women you meet on the street are for good, some are the agents of Lucifer—working for the marine kingdom. Marine kingdom is brutal when it comes to sexual activities upon this planet. The fallen ones, demons, and the agents of Satan binds the souls of men and women through sexual temptation and other sins.

Yes, the enemy has a legal right over you when you are leading your life outside the perfect will of God. Many experience strange dreams—sleeping with all kinds of people in their dreams. Usually the demons will transform themselves as the angel of light coming to you through the face of your family members, friends, past lovers, colleagues etc. in dreams to have intercourse with you.

The more they sleep with you, the more they drain your spiritual power. And you will find that many men and women have spiritual kids with these demons of the water without their knowledge. I am talking from experience. I struggled a lot with the powers of the water. Water realm is a kingdom itself, it's a spiritual world of its kind, however, a replica of what we see in this world in an advanced way.

Thus, things like immorality, adultery, lusts, fornication and the likes, are the fiery weapon of this kingdom to mankind. To be delivered, apart from renouncing and denouncing prayer, you have to embark on a journey of spiritual warfare. You will have to fight a good fight of faith for your freedom. The Holy Spirit of God is your back up. God is the king of mighty weapons.

Jesus Christ gave men and women who believe authority over demons. You have to know the Word and follow the principles of God. Some demons will only come out through intense prayers, and fasting. These are stubborn and rebellious spirit—water spirits.

I have to talk about marine powers because they rule this world. This world is covered by seas; the seas are larger than land area. The fall of Lucifer was before mankind. Genesis does not start with the fall of Lucifer; it starts with the first man Adam.

Revelation 12:9 And the great dragon was cast out, that old serpent, called the Devil, and Satan, which deceiveth the whole world: he was cast out into the earth, and his

angels were cast out with him.

Revelation 12:12 Therefore rejoice, ye heavens, and ye that dwell in them. Woe to the

inhabiters of the earth and of the sea! for the devil is come down unto you, having great wrath, because he knoweth that he hath but a short time.

The inhibiters of the earth and of the sea are under the attack of the enemy. The beautiful things is that through the blood of Jesus we overcome. The blood has the deliverance power to translate you from darkness to light, from powerless to power, from impurity to Holiness. The power is in the blood of Christ. Claim the power that comes through Christ you shall conquer.

Revelation 12:11 And they overcame him by the blood of the Lamb, and by the word of
their testimony; and they loved not their lives unto the death.

I have to say that from this scripture, we overcome by three things. Firstly, by the blood of the lamb, secondly, by the word of our testimony, when we testify about what Christ has done on the cross and in our lives, and lastly, by not loving our lives unto death, this basically means we forsake the worldly things and carry the cross—living the life of the cross that Christ has died for. He died so that we can live. He died so that we live through his spirit. He died so that we can become what He died for, and that is, and overcoming victorious life in spirit and truth, in all things.

Spirit, soul and Body.

There is the law of spirit that lead to life. And the law of flesh that lead to death. The spirit and soul does not die but lives forever. The body dies as it temporal. Therefore, when you concern your life with the spiritual life in Christ, His spirit quickens your spirit man, and allow you rise above challenges and temptations that comes through life.

The spirit of God is that mighty spirit that resurrected Jesus Christ. When this spirit bears witness to your spirit man, you will always be inspired to continue with the faith journey and able to stand against the wiles of the enemy.

Once in the vision of the night, I saw the enemy, Satan, studying the bible diligently, with a serious focus I haven't seen before. My question is that, if the Devil and his demons study the bible so that they can deceive us, who are we?

If the kingdom of the enemy knows about the power of the Word, we should likewise not neglect the Word. This generation is lazy to study, it's rare for one to spend at least an hour on the Word.

The Word of God is the life force of God. The Word of God is the DNA of God. The enemy knows how lazy we are when it comes to study. Thus, false teachers and prophets are followed more than true ones.

Following after the Spirit and the Word will lead us into victory. As I have said, we are the end time army of the Lord.

When your soaked in the glory of God, there would be no time for the lifestyle of immorality. When the body and the soul are subjected under the leadership of the Holy Spirit, it births the fruits of the spirits such as self-control, love, humility, and meekness.

22 But the fruit of the Spirit is love, joy, peace, longsuffering, gentleness, goodness, faith,

23 Meekness, temperance: against such there is no law.
Galatians 5:22-23.

Guard your heart.

G uard your heart. The issues of life come from your heart. Guarding your heart means to be conscious of everything that you allow in your space. What you sow, you eventually reap. There is a time for sowing, and a time for harvesting.

For instance, if you keep on watching horrific movies, slowly but surely you will start walking in fear. Let's talk about pornography, once you start, you will never stop. And it will drain your spiritual energy.

To walk in purity is to flee from an atmosphere that offers us carnal or fleshy gratification outside the will of God. Purity and self-control works hand in hand. Some things do not need prayers. But they need self-control. Like anger, we all get angry, even Jesus got angry, but it's how you deal with your anger. There is no amount of prayer that will stop anger unless it is demonic.

Even some prayer where you ask God to protect you from sinning, it is a vain prayer because He did that by the death of Christ on the cross. The cross of Jesus is the emblem of redemption, forgiveness and salvation for all mankind who believes.

1 Thessalonians 4:3 - *"For this is the will of God, even your sanctification, that ye should abstain from fornication."*

Paul here talk about abstinence from fornication. Abstinence is a self-denial or self-discipline. It is a firm decision that you make to stay pure and to work for the common good of the will of God.

In variety of things, we can discipline ourselves. There is a law of the flesh, and the law of spirit. it is either you follow the law of the flesh or the law of the spirit. men and women of old walked in holiness because they made a choice to. In all things, we have a choice. Not all things require prayers but spiritual wisdom, knowledge and understanding.

In my family I have seen the pattern of anger taking its tall. Something that is hereditary is demonic. That is why we have generation curses. Like Moses, his anger was generational. It started with his great ancestor, Levi. He could not be allowed into the promise land because his anger got in away.

I also at one point received the Word from the Lord to control anger. Anger is an emotion that can be controlled when you are subjected under the authority of the Holy Spirit. how many Christian believers are angry on the road when there traffic? Some things need self-control just like sexual lusts, fornication or adultery.

God has provided us a way to defeat temptations. Temptations will be there but by the grace of the Lord God through His son Jesus Christ we shall conquer—and come out the other side victorious.

7 And it came to pass after these things, that his master's wife cast her eyes upon Joseph; and she said, Lie with me.

8 But he refused, and said unto his master's wife, Behold, my master wotteth not what is with me in the house, and he hath committed all that he hath

to my hand;

9 There is none greater in this house than I; neither hath he kept back any thing from me but thee, because thou art his wife: how then can I do this great

wickedness, and sin against God?

10 And it came to pass, as she spake to Joseph day by day, that he hearkened not unto her, to lie by her, or to be with her.

11 And it came to pass about this time, that Joseph went into the house to do

his business; and there was none of the men of the house there within.

12 And she caught him by his garment, saying, Lie with me: and he left his garment in her hand, and fled, and got him out.

Genesis 39:7-12.

Joseph was loyal to God first, and second, to his master. He said *"how then can I do this great wickedness, and sin against God?"*. This is someone who is aware of the hand of God in his life—attributing everything unto God. The God-conscious someone who will ask "What will God think" when attempting to do something that is contrary to the will of God.

The Potiphar's wife daily begged and nagged Joseph to sleep with her. Apostle Paul was looking at the life of Joseph when he wrote about fleeing from youthful lusts, and from sexual immorality. In most of his letters, he touched upon the issue of morality within the believers.

1 Corinthians 6:18 *- "Flee fornication. Every sin that a man doeth is without the body; but he that committeth fornication sinneth against his own body."*

We can see that some things do not needs our prayer but to flee from them. We flee from the worldly things to avoid temptation. As we are looking at the issue of lust, the more we allow the word of the Lord to be the dominating factor in our lives, there more we will be on our way to victory. When the Word is not in full capacity in you, you spirit man would not be that strong to resist the temptation. The most important aspect of your being is your spirit man.

In my family, during spring we do what we call spring cleaning. It is basically a deep cleaning that normally you wouldn't do like cleaning all the rooms in the house, doing laundry, changing paint of the house, doing the yard etc.

Because spring is a season of new life. Dead trees come to life. It is a new season of new beginning. It is basically a new year in our African culture. By observation nature comes to life, it is a birth of new life, a new nature.

I am linking this analogy to a new life in spirit that comes through spiritual cleansing. As much as there is physical cleansing, there is also spiritual cleansing. A new life in spirit birthed by Jesus Christ himself. A new creature modeled by the working of the Holy Spirit. The scripture says "As He is in heaven, so are we on this earth".

The Levites priest in the covenant of Moses, cleansed the Israelites through the blood of animals. Without the blood of goats, rams, or cows, there will not be a spiritual cleansing. A one in need of cleansing would take with him or her an animal sacrifice to the ordained priest to be burned on an altar and the blood of the animal in the basin would be sprinkled upon the person. It is written in the books of Leviticus and numbers.

After this rituals, an individual is pronounced clean, forgiven, or blessed. The scripture in the book of Hebrew 9:22 says "Without the shedding of blood, there is no remission of sins". Blessed are we who are continuously cleansed by the precious blood of the lamb. The blood does not only purify us but lead us into victory in all things.

As we are spirit, soul and body, your spirit is fed by spiritual food. There is spiritual food, spiritual clothes and spiritual place for your inner man. Spiritual food is the Word of God, spiritual clothes is the garment of salvation, garment of praise, while spiritual place is the place you be when you are in Christ. Christ is in the heavenly places, therefore, you are in Him in the heavenly even though you are on this earth.

Ephesians 1:6 And hath raised us up together, and made us sit together in heavenly

places in Christ Jesus:

Seeing ourselves from this spiritual point of view, will give us confidence and boldness to win every battle that is against us. Many are battling addictions, temptations or various attacks from the marine kingdom, approaching the battle as we are seated with Christ in heavenly is the greatest victory lab of the mind.

If you picture yourself in heaven as you are, you wouldn't be defeated and conquered by the enemy with his evil missiles against the body. against the body, the enemy attacks us with sicknesses and diseases, be it through food or through sexual immorality.

Sex outside marriage will always come with serious repercussions. There are many you are wounded in spirit through wrong attachments. There are many who are carrying different personalities in their body. many are experiencing misfortune and lack, unbeknown of where the attack comes from.

Men and women with self-control always fulfils their God given destinies. Satan sexualized this world to kill dreams of men and women. These days, the world is chasing after the flesh more than Christ. As it is written that in the last days, there shall be a falling away.

The battle starts in the mind. You beat the demon of the mind; you win in your walk. There are billions of demons on this planet and their sole mission is to deceive the believers. They hate believers with deep passion as they know the power of a sincere prayer that come out of the heart of a Christian.

Your body is the temple. In spirit, your body is a house. Cleanse the house with the Word of God. Cleanse the house with a prayer lifestyle, fasting, worship, praise etc. these are the weapon of spirits—the swords that bring shame in the kingdom of darkness. Magnify the Lord with your tongue. Speak victory talks at all time, even if you feel defeated, speak positivity in your life.

Even if you feel distant to the Lord "The Lord is your shepherd" "The Lord is your light" "The Lord has become my salvation". He has translated many from darkness to light. There is nothing impossible to God. Since He broke the yoke of slavery through the hand of Moses to the Israelites, He shall also do the same.

Avoid tempting situation.

1 Corinthians 7:2 - *"Nevertheless, to avoid fornication, let every man have his own wife, and let every woman have her own husband."*

As a youth, it is a call to flee from fornication. Men and women are to avoid fornication through marriage. Marriage is a pure will of God. And a safe place for children to be born in. You can see many damaged children who are born out of marriage. There is always an intense deliverance needed if you are a man or women brought up through fornication. It is not God's plan.

More like an individual who doesn't know the whereabouts of his or her father, there are certain blessings in life he or she will miss. God is gracious, however, the blessings of the father to his or her children is important. In this day and age of feminism, the fatherhood is still important. Children with no father figure in their life are more prone to illicit behavior than those with fathers. Majority of them struggle with their identity.

Colossians 3:5 - *"Mortify therefore your members which are upon the earth; fornication, uncleanness, inordinate affection, evil concupiscence, and covetousness, which is idolatry."*

It is pretty clear that not all men and women will give into marriage. It is a choice for many to whether decide if they want marriage or not. Some people are more career oriented. Some want to but due to financial constrains are unable to. Some are the victims of horrible relationship and marriage and no longer want to bid anymore.

In all of these, we are to mortify our members, which is our body. To keep your body under subjection of the Holy Spirit. You kill the flesh through self-discipline and self-control. An individual who is zealous about the things of God can do this through the quickening of the spirit man by Jesus Christ's spirit.

Even in the age of grace and mercy, you still have to keep yourself pure. Holiness is a choice. He said "Be ye Holy, for I am Holy". Holiness shall see the face of the Lord. Already we are the righteousness of God in Christ. Submit your consciousness and sub-consciousness under the will of God, under the banner of the Holy Spirit.

The heading of this chapter is *avoiding tempting situations*. There are various things that believers can avoid to keep themselves away from temptations. However, temptation itself is not a sin, sin is what you do after being tempted. We all know that watching pornography lead to masturbation and other illicit sexual behavior. And it does not matter whether one is married or not. The effect is till the same.

Here are few things you can avoid;
Sexual content on social media.
Pornographic websites.
Sensual films, television series etc.
Sexual explicit novels.
Over-Sexualized music.
Sexual immoral friends.
Idleness in your life and more.

1 Corinthians 6:9 *- "Know ye not that the unrighteous shall not inherit the kingdom of God? Be not deceived: neither fornicators, nor idolaters, nor adulterers, nor effeminate, nor abusers of themselves with mankind."*
Jude 1:7 *- "Even as Sodom and Gomorrha, and the cities about them in like manner, giving themselves over to fornication, and going after strange flesh, are set forth for an example, suffering the vengeance of eternal fire."*

The sad real truth is that some of the leaders in the entertainment world have sold out to the Devil to produce the content that will lead many astray. The enemy knows the power of sex, and how sex can sell the whole nation, he therefore, propagate for sexual revolution. And it is working throughout the whole world, they will laugh at your face if you come with the sentiments like "Sex before marriage".

Music is inspired by fallen angels and demons. Blockbusters are channeled from other dimensions of other universes. If you look at the last theme of the movie industry is alien based, marine kingdom based—pushing the old luciferin agenda. Record labels that hold majority of top artists in this world are owned by freemasons. It is a total waste of time and energy consuming all the content from so called sold out artists.

One day I was on Amazon browsing the books of a certain Christian writer I admired, who is a successful best-selling author, then the spirit of the Lord told me that that individual sold his soul to the Devil. I couldn't fathom that idea.

God will never leave or forsake us. If we can listen to our intuition where most of the time spirit of God is at work within us, we will be delivered from the known and the unknown. As I always emphasize, the spirit of wisdom, knowledge, and understanding perfect us in Christ. And the discerning of spirits is one of the greatest give you will need in this last days.

Now it is serious battle between the children of light and the children of darkness. Satanic rituals used to be performed in secrets. Nowadays it is in your face, in schools, churches, departments, politics, media etc.

Indeed, it is the time of the falling away.

Revelation 17:4 - *"And the woman was arrayed in purple and scarlet colour, and decked with gold and precious stones and pearls, having a golden cup in her hand full of abominations and filthiness of her fornication."*

To build a Godly atmosphere in your life and at home to avoid lusts and stay away from sins like fornication, homosexuality, sexual immorality, and sexual lusts, start by immersing yourself in the Word of God.

The Bible is your guide to living a holy life. Read it every day and let its teachings shape your thoughts and actions. Psalm 119:11 says, "I have hidden your word in my heart that I might not sin against you." By filling your mind with Scripture, you protect yourself against temptation.

Surround yourself with positive influences. Choose friends who share your Christian values and who encourage you to live a pure life. Proverbs 13:20 reminds us, "Walk with the wise and become wise, for a companion of fools suffers harm."

Good friends can help you stay on the right path and avoid situations that might lead to sin. Attend church regularly and join Bible study groups to learn more about God's will for your life and gain strength from fellow believers.

At home, create an environment that honors God. Start with simple things like listening to Christian music, which can lift your spirit and keep your mind focused on God. Avoid media that promotes sexual immorality.

Be careful about what you watch on TV, the movies you choose, and the websites you visit. Philippians 4:8 says, "Finally, brothers and sisters, whatever is true, whatever is noble, whatever is right, whatever is pure, whatever is lovely, whatever is admirable—if anything is excellent or praiseworthy—think about such things." By choosing content that is wholesome, you protect your mind and heart from temptation.

Prayer is a powerful tool in your spiritual life. Pray every day, asking God to help you stay strong and resist the temptations that come your way. Be honest with God about your struggles and ask for His help to overcome them. James 5:16 says, "Therefore confess your sins to each other and pray for each other so that you may be healed. The prayer of a righteous person is powerful and effective." Through prayer, you can find strength and support to stay pure.

Set boundaries for yourself. Know your limits and be proactive in avoiding situations where you might be tempted. This might mean not spending time alone with someone you are attracted to or avoiding places where you know there will be a lot of temptations. 1 Corinthians 10:13 promises, "No temptation has overtaken you except what is common to mankind. And God is faithful; he will not let you be tempted beyond what you can bear. But when you are tempted, he will also provide a way out so that you can endure it." Setting boundaries is not about being fearful but about being wise and protecting yourself from falling into sin.

Encourage open and honest conversations in your home about these issues. Talk with your family about the importance of living a pure and holy life. Share your struggles and victories with each other and support one another in your journey. Proverbs 27:17 says, "As iron sharpens iron, so one person sharpens another." By being open and honest, you create a safe space where everyone feels comfortable seeking help and encouragement.

Finally, remember that building a Godly atmosphere takes time and effort, but it is worth it. Every step you take to honor God in your life and home helps you to avoid the pitfalls of lust and sexual immorality.

Keep your focus on God, surround yourself with positive influences, and make choices that honor Him. Romans 12:2 advises, "Do not conform to the pattern of this world, but be transformed by the renewing of your mind. Then you will be able to test and approve what God's will is—his good, pleasing and perfect will." In doing so, you will create an environment where it is easier to live a life that is pleasing to God and free from the bondage of sin.

1. Heavenly Father, I come before You seeking deliverance from sexual lust and temptations, In the name of Jesus.
2. I declare that my body is the temple of the Holy Spirit and I will honor God with my body, In the name of Jesus (1 Corinthians 6:19-20).
3. Lord, cleanse my mind from all impurities and renew my thoughts, In the name of Jesus (Romans 12:2).
4. I break every chain of sexual immorality that has bound me, In the name of Jesus (1 Corinthians 6:18).
5. I decree that no weapon formed against me shall prosper, and I condemn every tongue that rises against me in judgment, In the name of Jesus (Isaiah 54:17).
6. I declare that I am set free from the bondage of sin and death, In the name of Jesus (Romans 8:2).
7. I proclaim that I am a new creation in Christ, and old things have passed away, In the name of Jesus (2 Corinthians 5:17).
8. Lord, strengthen me to resist the devil, and he will flee from me, In the name of Jesus (James 4:7).
9. I take captive every thought and make it obedient to Christ, In the name of Jesus (2 Corinthians 10:5).
10. I decree that I am more than a conqueror through Him who loves me, In the name of Jesus (Romans 8:37).
11. Lord, create in me a clean heart and renew a right spirit within me, In the name of Jesus (Psalm 51:10).
12. I renounce every evil spirit of lust and perversion, In the name of Jesus (Mark 16:17).
13. I declare that I have the mind of Christ and the thoughts of purity and holiness, In the name of Jesus (1 Corinthians 2:16).
14. I plead the blood of Jesus over my mind, body, and spirit for

protection and cleansing, In the name of Jesus (Revelation 12:11).

15. I proclaim freedom from all generational curses of sexual sin, In the name of Jesus (Galatians 3:13).

16. Lord, guard my heart and my eyes from all forms of temptation, In the name of Jesus (Proverbs 4:23).

17. I declare that sin shall no longer have dominion over me, for I am under grace, In the name of Jesus (Romans 6:14).

18. I break the power of every spirit of pornography and sexual addiction, In the name of Jesus (Matthew 5:28).

19. I decree that I will walk in the Spirit and not fulfill the lust of the flesh, In the name of Jesus (Galatians 5:16).

20. Lord, empower me with Your Holy Spirit to live a life of purity and holiness, In the name of Jesus (Ephesians 5:18).

21. I proclaim that I am dead to sin and alive to God in Christ Jesus, In the name of Jesus (Romans 6:11).

22. I break every ungodly soul tie formed through past sexual relationships, In the name of Jesus (1 Corinthians 6:16).

23. I declare that I am clothed with the righteousness of Christ, In the name of Jesus (2 Corinthians 5:21).

24. Lord, fill me with Your love, which casts out all fear and sin, In the name of Jesus (1 John 4:18).

25. I decree that I will meditate on whatever is true, noble, right, pure, lovely, and admirable, In the name of Jesus (Philippians 4:8).

26. I proclaim that I am holy and blameless before You, Lord, In the name of Jesus (Ephesians 1:4).

27. I declare that I will set my mind on things above, not on earthly things, In the name of Jesus (Colossians 3:2).

28. I break the power of every spirit of seduction and Jezebel, In the name of Jesus (Revelation 2:20).

29. I decree that I am filled with the fruits of the Spirit, which

include self-control, In the name of Jesus (Galatians 5:22-23).

30. Lord, lead me not into temptation but deliver me from evil, In the name of Jesus (Matthew 6:13).

31. I declare that I am crucified with Christ and no longer live, but Christ lives in me, In the name of Jesus (Galatians 2:20).

32. I break every spirit of shame and guilt over past sins, In the name of Jesus (Romans 8:1).

33. I proclaim that Your grace is sufficient for me, and Your power is made perfect in my weakness, In the name of Jesus (2 Corinthians 12:9).

34. I declare that I will flee youthful lusts and pursue righteousness, faith, love, and peace, In the name of Jesus (2 Timothy 2:22).

35. Lord, set a guard over my mouth and keep watch over the door of my lips, In the name of Jesus (Psalm 141:3).

36. I decree that I will walk in the light as You are in the light, and have fellowship with You, In the name of Jesus (1 John 1:7).

37. I declare that I will not conform to the patterns of this world but be transformed by the renewing of my mind, In the name of Jesus (Romans 12:2).

38. I proclaim that I have been washed, sanctified, and justified in the name of the Lord Jesus Christ and by the Spirit of our God, In the name of Jesus (1 Corinthians 6:11).

39. I break the power of every spirit of idolatry and impurity, In the name of Jesus (Colossians 3:5).

40. I decree that I am a child of God, and I will live in the freedom and purity that Christ has given me, In the name of Jesus (John 8:36).

Spiritual Warfare: Overcoming Sexual Lust, Temptations, and Sexual Demons

Types of Spiritual Warfare

Spiritual warfare involves a range of strategies and actions designed to confront and defeat the powers of darkness that seek to influence our lives. Here are some key types of spiritual warfare to consider:

1. **Prayer and Fasting**: These are foundational tools in spiritual warfare. Prayer connects us with God's power and wisdom, while fasting helps us deny the flesh and focus on spiritual matters. Jesus emphasized the power of prayer and fasting when dealing with difficult spiritual battles (Matthew 17:21).

2. **The Word of God**: Using Scripture as a weapon is crucial. Jesus Himself used Scripture to combat Satan's temptations in the wilderness (Matthew 4:1-11). Memorizing and declaring relevant Bible verses can help to reinforce our resolve and remind us of God's promises.

3. **Confession and Repentance**: Regularly confessing our sins and repenting keeps our hearts pure before God. James 5:16 states, "Therefore confess your sins to each other and pray for each other so that you may be healed. The prayer of a righteous person is powerful and effective."

4. **Praise and Worship**: These can be powerful tools against the enemy. Worshiping God shifts our focus from our problems to His greatness, and it can break strongholds (2 Chronicles 20:22).

5. **Binding and Loosing**: Jesus gave us authority to bind and loose spiritual forces (Matthew 18:18). We can bind demonic influences that seek to tempt us and loose God's blessings and protection over our lives.

6. **Accountability and Fellowship**: Engaging in regular fellowship with other believers and maintaining accountability can provide support and encouragement in the fight against sin (Hebrews 10:24-25).

The Need for Spiritual Warfare

Sexual lust, temptations, and sexual demons are powerful forces that can lead to destructive behaviors and separation from God. Engaging in spiritual warfare is necessary because:

1. **Spiritual Battles Are Real**: Ephesians 6:12 reminds us that "our struggle is not against flesh and blood, but against the rulers, against the authorities, against the powers of this dark world and against the spiritual forces of evil in the heavenly realms."

2. **Protection and Deliverance**: Spiritual warfare provides a means for us to seek God's protection and deliverance from these forces. Psalm 91 speaks of God's promise to protect those who dwell in His presence.

3. **Living a Holy Life**: We are called to live holy lives, free from the bondage of sin. 1 Thessalonians 4:3-4 says, "It is God's will that you should be sanctified: that you should avoid sexual immorality; that each of you should learn to control your own body in a way that is holy and honorable."

From Defeat to Victory: A Practical Approach

Moving from defeat to victory in the area of sexual lust and temptation involves several practical steps:

1. **Acknowledgement and Confession**: Admit your struggles to God and confess your sins. 1 John 1:9 promises, "If we confess our sins, he is faithful and just and will forgive us our sins and purify us from all unrighteousness."

2. **Renew Your Mind**: Commit to renewing your mind daily with God's Word. Romans 12:2 instructs, "Do not conform to the pattern of this world, but be transformed by the renewing of your mind."

3. **Prayer and Fasting**: Set aside regular times for prayer and fasting to seek God's strength and guidance.

4. **Use Scripture**: Memorize and declare scriptures that address purity and strength against temptation. For instance, 1 Corinthians 10:13, "No temptation has overtaken you except what is common to mankind. And God is faithful; he will not let you be tempted beyond what you can bear."

5. **Establish Boundaries**: Set practical boundaries to avoid situations that may lead to temptation. This could include internet filters, avoiding certain places, or ending unhealthy relationships.

6. **Accountability Partner**: Find a trusted friend or mentor who can provide accountability, prayer support, and encouragement.

7. **Engage in Worship**: Regularly participate in worship to shift your focus from your struggles to God's power and majesty.

8. **Seek Professional Help**: If necessary, seek help from a Christian counselor who can provide strategies and support in overcoming these issues.

9. **Stay in Fellowship**: Regularly attend church and participate in small groups to build strong relationships with other believers who can support you in your journey.

10. **Trust in God's Grace**: Finally, trust in God's grace and mercy. Philippians 1:6 assures us, "being confident of this, that he who began a good work in you will carry it on to completion until the day of Christ Jesus."

By consistently applying these principles, you can move from a place of defeat to a place of victory, living a life that honors God and is free from the bondage of sexual lust and temptations.

The Power of Meditating on Scripture

Meditating on Scripture is a transformative practice that empowers believers to overcome sexual lust, homosexuality, sexual demons, adultery, and other sins. When we meditate on God's Word, we allow its truths to penetrate our hearts and minds, shaping our thoughts, attitudes, and actions. Psalm 1:2-3 highlights the blessings of this practice: "But whose delight is in the law of the LORD, and who meditates on his law day and night. That person is like a tree planted by streams of water, which yields its fruit in season and whose leaf does not wither—whatever they do prospers." This passage illustrates that those who consistently meditate on Scripture are spiritually nourished and resilient against the attacks of sin.

One of the key benefits of meditating on Scripture is the renewal of our minds. Romans 12:2 urges us, "Do not conform to the pattern of this world, but be transformed by the renewing of your mind." By continually focusing on God's Word, we replace worldly and sinful thoughts with pure and holy ones. This mental transformation is essential in combating sexual lust and temptations, as it equips us to recognize and reject sinful desires.

Moreover, meditating on Scripture strengthens our resolve to live righteously. Psalm 119:11 declares, "I have hidden your word in my heart that I might not sin against you." When God's Word is deeply embedded in our hearts, it acts as a safeguard against sin. In moments of temptation, the Holy Spirit can bring to our remembrance the Scriptures we have meditated upon, empowering us to resist. For instance, when tempted by sexual immorality, recalling verses like 1 Corinthians 6:18, "Flee from sexual immorality," can fortify our determination to remain pure.

Additionally, meditation on Scripture provides clarity and guidance. Proverbs 6:23 says, "For this command is a lamp, this teaching is a light, and correction and instruction are the way to life." The Bible offers clear instructions on how to live a life that honors God, including how to handle sexual temptations. By meditating on these teachings, we gain wisdom and discernment, enabling us to navigate challenging situations without falling into sin.

Furthermore, meditating on Scripture fosters a deeper relationship with God, which is foundational for overcoming sin. As we spend time in God's Word, we grow in our knowledge and love for Him. This intimacy fuels our desire to please Him and strengthens our commitment to holiness. Knowing that our bodies are temples of the Holy Spirit (1 Corinthians 6:19-20), we are motivated to maintain purity and avoid actions that grieve Him.

The Power of Fasting

Fasting is a powerful spiritual discipline that, when combined with prayer and meditation on Scripture, can lead to victory over sexual lust, homosexuality, sexual demons, adultery, and other sins. Fasting involves abstaining from food, or certain types of food, for a specified period to focus more intently on spiritual matters. This practice is not just about self-denial but about seeking God with greater intensity and purpose. Isaiah 58:6 emphasizes the liberating power of fasting: "Is not this the kind of fasting I have chosen: to loose the chains of injustice and untie the cords of the yoke, to set the oppressed free and break every yoke?"

One of the significant benefits of fasting is that it helps to subdue the flesh and its desires. When we fast, we deny our physical appetites, which strengthens our ability to resist other bodily temptations, including sexual lust. Galatians 5:16 instructs us to "walk by the Spirit, and you will not gratify the desires of the flesh." Fasting enhances our spiritual sensitivity and reliance on the Holy Spirit, making it easier to overcome fleshly desires.

Fasting also breaks spiritual strongholds and demonic influences. Jesus taught that some forms of spiritual bondage require fasting for deliverance. In Matthew 17:21, He said, "But this kind does not go out except by prayer and fasting." This principle applies to overcoming powerful sexual demons and addictions. By fasting, we engage in a deeper level of spiritual warfare, inviting God's power to break these strongholds.

Moreover, fasting heightens our spiritual awareness and draws us closer to God. James 4:8 promises, "Come near to God and he will come near to you." During a fast, our heightened spiritual focus allows us to experience God's presence more profoundly, which strengthens our resolve to live righteously. This intimacy with God empowers us to reject sexual sins and embrace purity.

Fasting also aligns our will with God's will. As we humble ourselves through fasting, we become more receptive to God's guidance and correction. This humility is crucial in overcoming sins like adultery and sexual lust. Psalm 35:13 says, "I humbled myself with fasting." In this state of humility, we are more open to repenting of our sins and receiving God's grace for transformation.

In addition, fasting often leads to a breakthrough in areas of persistent struggle. When combined with prayer, fasting can bring clarity, revelation, and direction from God. This spiritual breakthrough is essential for overcoming entrenched patterns of sin. Joel 2:12-13 calls us to return to God with fasting, weeping, and mourning, promising restoration and blessing.

Practically, moving from defeat to victory involves incorporating regular periods of fasting into our spiritual disciplines. Start with a manageable duration, such as a one-day fast, and gradually extend the period as you grow more comfortable with the practice. During the fast, dedicate specific times for prayer, reading, and meditating on Scripture, focusing on passages that address purity and holiness.

In conclusion, meditating on Scripture and fasting are powerful tools in the believer's arsenal for defeating sexual lust, homosexuality, sexual demons, adultery, and other sins. These disciplines renew our minds, subdue our flesh, break spiritual strongholds, and draw us closer to God. By consistently engaging in these practices, we can move from a place of defeat to a place of victory, living lives that honor God and reflect His holiness.

The Power of Spiritual Worship, Praise, and Thanksgiving

Spiritual worship, praise, and thanksgiving are potent weapons in the battle against sexual lusts and other temptations. These practices redirect our focus from the desires of the flesh to the glory of God, transforming our hearts and minds in the process. Incorporating worship, praise, and thanksgiving into daily life can fortify our spirits and provide the strength needed to overcome sinful inclinations.

The Power of Worship

Worship is a powerful act of devotion that places God at the center of our lives. It is an expression of love, reverence, and adoration for God, which brings us into His presence. Jesus said in John 4:24, "God is spirit, and his worshipers must worship in the Spirit and in truth." True worship engages our hearts and minds, aligning us with God's will and purpose.

When we engage in worship, we invite the Holy Spirit to fill us and guide us. This divine presence helps us resist temptations and remain steadfast in our commitment to purity. Worship shifts our focus from worldly desires to heavenly realities, reminding us of our identity in Christ. Romans 12:1 urges us, "Therefore, I urge you, brothers and sisters, in view of God's mercy, to offer your bodies as a living sacrifice, holy and pleasing to God—this is your true and proper worship." By presenting our bodies as living sacrifices in worship, we dedicate ourselves to God and reject sexual immorality.

The Power of Praise

Praise is a powerful declaration of God's greatness and goodness. It is an act of faith that acknowledges God's sovereignty and power over all circumstances, including our struggles with sin. Psalm 150:6 says, "Let everything that has breath praise the Lord. Praise the Lord." When we praise God, we proclaim His attributes, celebrate His works, and affirm our trust in Him.

Praising God can break spiritual strongholds and change the atmosphere around us. Acts 16:25-26 recounts how Paul and Silas praised God in prison, leading to a miraculous earthquake that freed them. Similarly, praising God can release us from the chains of sexual lust and temptation. It lifts our spirits, renews our minds, and strengthens our faith. By focusing on God's power and goodness, we become less susceptible to the lies and deceptions of the enemy.

The Power of Thanksgiving

Thanksgiving is the act of expressing gratitude to God for His blessings, grace, and mercy. It fosters a spirit of contentment and joy, which are crucial in combating the discontent and dissatisfaction that often lead to sexual sin. 1 Thessalonians 5:18 instructs, "Give thanks in all circumstances; for this is God's will for you in Christ Jesus." A thankful heart is a protected heart, less likely to seek fulfillment in sinful ways.

Giving thanks reminds us of God's faithfulness and provision. It shifts our focus from what we lack to what we have in Christ. This shift in perspective helps us resist the allure of sexual temptations by recognizing the sufficiency of God's blessings. Philippians 4:6-7 encourages us, "Do not be anxious about anything, but in every situation, by prayer and petition, with thanksgiving, present your requests to God. And the peace of God, which transcends all understanding, will guard your hearts and your minds in Christ Jesus." Thanksgiving brings peace and guards our hearts against sinful desires.

Practical Steps for Daily Worship, Praise, and Thanksgiving

1. **Start Your Day with Worship**: Begin each day with a time of worship, setting your heart and mind on God. Sing songs, read Psalms, or simply speak words of adoration to God.

2. **Incorporate Praise Throughout Your Day**: Make a habit of

praising God throughout your day. Whenever you face a temptation or struggle, take a moment to praise God for His power and faithfulness.

3. **Keep a Gratitude Journal**: Write down things you are thankful for each day. Reflecting on God's blessings can help shift your focus from negative thoughts and temptations to positive affirmations of God's goodness.

4. **Use Scripture in Your Praise and Thanksgiving**: Meditate on and declare scriptures that celebrate God's attributes and promises. Passages like Psalm 103:1-5 and Philippians 4:8 are great places to start.

5. **Create a Worshipful Environment**: Surround yourself with worship music and other uplifting media. This can help maintain a spirit of worship and praise throughout your day.

6. **Join a Worship Community**: Engage regularly with a church or small group where you can worship, praise, and give thanks with other believers. Fellowship strengthens your resolve and provides accountability.

7. **Pray with Thanksgiving**: When you pray, always include elements of thanksgiving. Thank God for past victories over sin and trust Him for future victories.

By making worship, praise, and thanksgiving daily habits, we create a spiritual atmosphere that is conducive to purity and holiness. These practices draw us closer to God, fortify our spirits, and provide the strength needed to overcome sexual lusts and other temptations. Through consistent and heartfelt worship, praise, and thanksgiving, we can experience the transforming power of God in our lives and walk in victory over sin.

Notes.

A Teaching Article by Peter Horrobin International Director of Ellel Ministries.

Don't miss out!

Visit the website below and you can sign up to receive emails whenever Johannes Tefo publishes a new book. There's no charge and no obligation.

https://books2read.com/r/B-A-UEZX-GMKJD

BOOKS 2 READ

Connecting independent readers to independent writers.

Did you love *Sexual Lust, Demons, And Impurity*? Then you should read *A Women's Guide To Spiritual Warfare*[1] by Johannes Tefo!

[2]

We are in the end time season whereby the invisible kingdoms are manifesting more and more. And in this season, unshakable faith and prayer has to be the bedrock of every Christian. This *Women Spiritual Warfare Guide* is tailord specifically for women to go in the frontilne to fight for their marriages, children, family, community and the world at large to be a peaceful place for their seeds.

A women's seed is at rock bottom to be sallowed up by the kingdom of darkness. As long as we know who we are in Christ, no weapon formed against us shall prosper. But that does not mean that the devil will leave us alone. It takes a strong faith to resist the wiles and devices of the en-

---

1. https://books2read.com/u/4XwRde

2. https://books2read.com/u/4XwRde

emy. This guide came at the perfect time for you to see the devil out of your home. It is filled with practical steps that will lead you to nothing but victory.

Add this book to your collection, your life would never be the same.

Also by Johannes Tefo

Family spiritual Warfare Books

Generational Curses And Spiritual Warfare: Spiritual Strategies & Principles Of Victory Against Evil Strongholds

Youth's Guide To Spiritual Warfare

A Women's Guide To Spiritual Warfare

Standalone

Deliver Your Soul From Evil

Overcoming Spirit Of Stagnation

The 24: Prophetic Word For This Season 2024 And Beyond

Michael For Warfare

Territorial Spirits: Overcome Evil Strongholds in Your Life And Take Over Your Community With Strategic Warfare And Winning Prayers

Prayers Against Suicide Spirit

Spiritual Warfare When Enough is Enough

Identity In Christ

Prayers Against Satanic Networks

The Workplace You Need: Spiritual Warfare Prayers That Silence Evil Powers At Your Workplace.

Deliverance From Mind Control: Be Free And Delivered From Every Marine Demons Of Mind Control

Times Getting Hard: Scriptures Of Comfort For Hard Days

Battle In The Sea: How To Tackle Spiritual Warfare And Win The Battle

Freedom: Deliverance Of Souls From Captivity

A Dedicated Prayer Lifestyle: Simple Tips To Effective Prayer Lifestyle

Deliverance From Sexual Dreams

Sexual Lust, Demons, And Impurity

Redefined By Fire: Unleashing The Power Of The Holy Spirit Within.

About the Author

Before he started writing Christian books, Johannes got a graduate degree in Film and Television from university of Johannesburg. After that, just to shake things up, he went to equip himself with religious studies, particularly Christianity, just to have knack about the world beyond the curtains of time. And how this body of Christ has transformed millions of people around the world, not neglecting how sadly the movement has been persecuted from time to time. He now writes full time.